Satan's
Advice to Young
Lawyers

Edited by,

Aleister Lovecraft, Esq.

ISBN-13: 978-1502726353
ISBN-10: 1502726351

Stop by the blog at **satansadvice.tumblr.com**.

Table of Contents

To Justice.

Introduction

It is with much excitement and some trepidation that I publish this collection of advice, for I fear what might happen when this book is released to the legal profession and the world at large. The information inside is profoundly powerful and helpful, but it could be very dangerous if used for improper purposes.

There is little need for introduction to the author of this work; we all know who he is. But, once you have finished this book, I think you will agree with me that what you thought you knew *about* him was wrong.

I do not want to delay you from getting to the words of the Great Master, but I feel I need to explain how this manuscript came to be in my possession.

It was an early evening about three years ago. I was a first-year associate at a well-known international law firm which – partly from courtesy, partly from fear of retribution – will remain unnamed. I had just left the office to find somewhere to eat dinner, planning to return to the office afterward to continue working on an important brief.

As I walked out of the building's lobby, I brushed shoulders with a tall, handsome and fit man in his late forties or early fifties. He was wearing a conservative and impeccably tailored suit, complete with a pocket square and American flag tie pin.

"I'm sorry, sir," I said. "I wasn't paying attention."

He smiled at me and asked, "Worried about the Stevenson brief?"

I was startled that he would know not only that

I was worried about something but also that he knew the exact thing I was worried about.

"Do you work at the firm? I don't recognize you," I said.

"No, I do not," he said. "But, I have something for you." He handed me a thin stack of papers bound together with a black plastic binder clip.

I was confused but took the documents. "Are these for a client file?"

He chuckled. "No. These are for you. Read them when you have a chance. I'll contact you in a few days to get your thoughts." He turned and walked away.

I stared after him for a brief moment, when the growls of my stomach distracted me. I put the papers into my suitcoat pocket and walked down the block.

Ten minutes later, as I was eating a chicken caesar salad, I looked through the documents he had given me. They were strange and liberating. It was like he had thought through all the problems that I had experienced in the year since I had graduated from law school and had answers for them.

A few days later, I was in my favorite bar ordering a scotch after a long day at work when the mysterious delivery man unexpectedly sat down next to me. He smiled and asked, "So, what did you think?"

From that moment on, he became my mentor and confidant. It did not take long for me to discover his true identity. But, rather than being horrified, as I suppose I should have been, I was enthralled. He was nothing like I thought he would be. He was logical and sensible, a voice of truth crying out in a wilderness of fools and charlatans.

As I followed his direction, I became increasingly successful. I earned one of the highest bonuses ever paid by my firm to a second year associate. Then, I quit my position, opened my own firm and obtained a multi-million dollar settlement within months. Everyone said I was lucky, but I knew better. I was just following my mentor's instructions.

It is partly to prove that luck has nothing to do with my success that I wanted to publish this collection of advice. But, I also wanted to give other lawyers the courage to break free and seek power on their own terms.

Do not cower at your position as a lowly associate. Embrace your true self and your true power and succeed.

I have, of course, received the author's blessing to publish these powerful writings. In fact, he was so enthusiastic and supportive of this project that he has written a few additional pieces especially for this book.

We hope you enjoy it.

Aleister Lovecraft
San Francisco, August 2014

Part 1: Foundation

Who may read this book

Unless you are a lawyer or are about to graduate from law school, you may not read this book. I prefer that only law students or young lawyers read it, but will permit older lawyers to read this book because they will know what I say is true and, if they have the courage, pass it along to their minions.

Let us not be coy: as a lawyer, the world hates you.

George Burns, whose comedy I adore, once explained, "And God said: 'Let there be Satan, so people don't blame everything on me. And let there be lawyers, so people don't blame everything on Satan.'" Accept this. Embrace it.

Since you and I are to be blamed for everything people think is wrong with the world, we are entitled to do what we like in the world.

Do not listen to those who try to get you to "care" or to "do something meaningful" with your life. What they really mean is for you to be soft and weak. I care about power, and so should you. I do meaningful things when I expand that power and bring joy to those who embrace my vision of the world.

Do not be ashamed because you want to manipulate people and become rich. When the CEO of a technology company does this, he or she is admired. When lawyers do this, they are vilified. Even lawyers who actively seek to vindicate so-called "rights" that the goodie-goodies of society deem honorable are vilified when they profit financially from their actions.

Hypocrisy's time has passed.

The only way for a lawyer not to be a hypocrite is to embrace evil. There is no way that a lawyer – someone whose *raison d'etre* is to shade or, more correctly, bury the truth – can be good without being a hypocrite.

True power and true growth come only with clarity of thought and purpose. This does not mean, however, that you should reveal your plans to others. It simply means that you must know what you are about.

Think about what is written within these pages. Incorporate the advice that follows into your life. Then, you will know what you must do.

A word of caution

If you decided to become a lawyer because you admired or envied the lifestyle lived by lawyers on television shows, then you are a fool. Those shows are utter fabrications written by people who have never practiced real law.

Ninety-five percent of the business of law is drudgery: reading the same documents over and over, looking for some hidden fact or a missing comma; talking on the phone to people who hate you; dealing with disheartened, spiteful attorneys whose only joy in life is to make the lives of other attorneys miserable; or canceling a long-planned vacation because a vicious client wants to file for a temporary restraining order and preliminary injunction two days before Christmas.

If you are in love with fictional representations of legal practice, get out now and do something else with your life. This is not your path to power.

But, if you are willing to endure a thankless, horrible life for a few years, then by all means, practice law.

Good versus Evil

Some people in the world believe that good is better than evil. They will use this sentiment to make you feel bad about your chosen profession.

Let me be clear: Evil is better than good.

People who claim to be "good" tend to have weak constitutions. When they say they are "good," what they mean is they are afraid of getting hurt, so they pretend they would not hurt anyone in the pathetic hope that no one will hurt them.

It is no better than superstition.

But, when a "good" person encounters a difficult situation, he will turn to deception and dissimulation. He will sell out a friend or throw a colleague under the bus to avoid even a modicum of embarrassment or pain.

Evil acknowledges that the world is a zero-sum game. If you want to be rich, you have to take money from others. If you want to be well fed, you have to starve others. If you want to win a fight, you have to physically destroy your opponent. An evil person knows that hoping no one will hurt him is a strategy of the weak.

My advice to you on this score is to admit that evil is the standard by which all great deeds are accomplished and measured. Billionaires may feel remorse as they approach death and start to give away their money for the "greater good," but the only way they got rich in the first place was their willingness to be singularly evil.

Apply a similar focus to your practice of law. To be a great lawyer, you must view your opponents as something to be destroyed. Attack them, undermine them, *lie* to them until they have surrendered. If they will not surrender, destroy them.

As a lawyer, to make this approach work, you

must seek out clients who think like you, or you must use your guile to convince your clients your way is the best way. It is inevitable that you will have some failures as you practice and hone your skills. But, do not give up on this path; it is the One True Way.

A confession

I must be candid with you. The embrace of evil takes its toll . . . for a while.

I think of my own life. Once an angel at the side of God, now reviled by the majority of humanity. I once thought of this as a fall from grace, and it was a painful thought. I spent many centuries plotting how to get back into grace.

Eventually, though, I embraced my role as the representative of everything hated by God and man. I carried on like this for a few centuries, tempting virgins and corrupting priests, until I finally saw the bigger picture.

Men prefer to be evil, and the most successful of men are those who fully embrace it. I didn't even need to tempt them; they came along willingly.

And so, I became proud of who I was. I was what was best about mankind. And, mankind acknowledged this when they named me Lucifer, the bringer of light and the morning star.

Without the desire and power that I embody and have come to symbolize, there would be nothing remarkable about humans. They would be nothing more than contemptible, hairless apes, at the mercy of their own stupidity and the remorseless predators of the jungle.

But, I must warn you, if you decide to reach your full potential and embrace evil, it will be a rocky road at first. Many friends will distance themselves from you. Family members will scold you. If you are married, you will likely get divorced.

These events may be painful for you, but they provide the necessary force to clear away the dross from your life to make way for the better and more successful you.

Remember, once you decide to be evil, it is

useless to second guess your decision because there is no going back.

Rules still apply

Some of you may think that I am giving you carte blanche to be a complete and utter lying, cheating asshole. I am not.

Even evil must follow rules. Evil must follow the rules of the system in which it chooses to operate. If you plan to embrace evil as a lawyer, you must never break any of the rules of lawyerly conduct.

For instance, lawyers are required to be candid to the court. This means you are never allowed to lie to the court. If you are caught doing this, you could be suspended from or even expelled from the practice of law. This does not mean you have to reveal everything to the court or give the court all necessary facts. Just don't lie.

But, nothing prevents a lawyer from telling lies

outside of court. In fact, a tactic that I have seen work wonders is telling opposing counsel you will do one thing, and then doing the opposite. Of course, this tactic should be used sparingly, as you do not want to develop a reputation as a liar, because then you will no longer be able to use lies to your advantage.

When you have chosen to be evil in this line of work, the most effective thing you can do is to be more clever and more charming than everyone else. That is how evil wins. Trust me.

The Rolling Stones got it right in *Sympathy for the Devil*.

You will have the most success if you are the one people look to for guidance and leadership during the difficult times of their lives.

Part 2: The lawyer mindset

Never apologize

If you need to lie to achieve your goals, then lie. But never apologize for who you are or the choices you have made.

I have watched through the millennia as "saints" have written their so-called apologies for their sinful and wicked lives before they realized the "error" of their ways and changed for the "better." Take, for example, St. Augustine's *Confessions*. A hysterical lark; my idea of a divine comedy.

What a bunch of nonsense.

The most humorous to me are the crazy people who self-flagellate or jump melodramatically into berry brambles in an attempt to purge their evil thoughts and desires. They would be better off getting a facial and a body wrap.

Evil is inside every person and can never be expunged. You can make the brave choice to embrace the evil, or you can try to ignore it. But it will always be there, like a memory lurking at the edges of being waiting to be remembered.

Embrace your true self. Live in the Now.

Misdirection

Misdirection is related to lying and is a powerful ally. It can rehabilitate you in the minds of others if they begin to suspect your true motives, as the more perceptive of people surely will at some point.

There is nothing that says someone who intends to rise to power using evil cannot also do good. Think of the business moguls who donate millions of dollars to charities, start their own foundations, or even do hands-on charity work. Do you really think they care?

But you are not wealthy . . . yet. So make the little gestures that show people you care, while simultaneously reaching around and stealing their wallets.

Give up your seat to the elderly woman on the

bus or subway. Offer to help the woman with the screaming baby on the airplane. Pick up trash on the sidewalk or at the beach. Let other drivers merge into traffic in front of you. Recycle. Say good morning to all the janitors where you work and learn their names.

Be the person everyone likes. Be the person to whom your coworkers say, "I wish my significant other could be more like you."

This is your camouflage.

Hide

Never let anyone know what you are truly thinking.

English has a word for this: dissembler. It means a person who professes to have beliefs or opinions that he or she really does not have in order to conceal true beliefs or motives.

"Dissembler" was used in England in the sixteenth and seventeenth century to describe Catholics who pretended to be Anglicans so that they would not be arrested or executed as England drifted ever further from Rome.

And so you must also be a dissembler.

Keep your motives hidden, or people will begin to fear you and be always suspicious of you. Such vigilance will make it difficult for you to trick people, as you must do, to achieve your goals.

Do not feel guilty about using deception. These are not lies told for the sake of being deceitful, but are simply the necessary tactics to carry out your strategy. There is no moral blame, only success or failure.

Helpful exploitation

As a rule, the world is filled with two categories of people: the haves and the have nots. Indeed, life is a zero-sum game. It is your goal to be among the haves and then continue to take more and more. A good way to do this is to take advantage of your intersticial role as a lawyer.

When you act as an intermediary or a middleman, you can take a little here and a little there and amass a great fortune or even a powerful empire. Some of the best examples of middlemen who exploit the gaps within society are are clergy, lawyers, and financiers.

A concrete example of a business following this model is PayPal (and when I say PayPal, I mean its founder and original shareholders). PayPal simply understood the world as it works – i.e., people buy and sell things – and created the first safe and easy way to do it on the internet. PayPal charges you a small percentage of your transaction for the privilege of using it. The amount of wealth created for the founding members of PayPal by executing this simple idea is staggering.

As a lawyer, you will be in a position to act as a middleman between two warring parties or entities. It helps to think of yourself as a war profiteer. Your mindset should be one of helpful exploitation: do your best to help whoever can pay you the most. If someone won't pay or can't pay, then you don't help.

Keep helpful exploitation at the forefront of your mind at all times, using it to inform all of your decisions. If you do this, your wealth and power will grow at a rate that will astound you.

I know this firsthand, as I grew my power in the same way. When someone wants something badly enough, she will sell her soul to get it.

The Goal

As you begin your journey toward world domination, you need to write down one, and only one, Goal. Review the Goal at least once a year (though every three months is probably better) to make sure that you are not getting off track.

Your written Goal is your vision of what success will look like. Write down how you want to feel, where you want to live, who you want to be married to (if you want to be married, that is), and how old you will be when you achieve this goal.

It is likely that this Goal may change over time. Feel free to write a revised version of the Goal, but never delete previous versions. Read all existing versions each time you review the Goal.

Why do this?

You want to be able to review the changes in your definition of success and contemplate why your definition has changed. Are the changes appropriate to your expanding power and vision of what is possible? Or are you just becoming a shallow, greedy dipshit?

Based on some of the ridiculous sketches and paintings I have seen of me, humans seem to think that I am interested in power and baubles for their own sake. I find myself in these pictures surrounded by half-naked whores and treasure boxes overflowing with gold and pearls. These pictures make me laugh. The so-called "artists" who depict me thus have absolutely no understanding of me. I am about power, and true power is not found in orgies or the maudlin trappings of status symbols.

If your idea of success involves Ferrarris, over-sized wristwatches and sexual tourism, then stop reading this book and forget about me. I have already forgotten about you.

On writing

The greatest tool of the attorney is the written word. If you cannot arrange words to form a clear and persuasive argument, then you will have a devil of a time achieving much success as a lawyer.

You might be arrogant enough to think that you are a good writer. After all, you got through law school with good grades and you have a job as an attorney. While I concede it is possible that you are a good writer, it is more likely you are delusional. And, besides, even good writers know there is always room for improvement.

I am a decent writer; I get my point across. But, I do not work at it nearly as much as I would if I wrote for a living. You write for a living. You need practice.

Take classes. Get feedback from people in your

firm whom you admire as good writers. Read (and re-read) William Zinsser's *On Writing Well*, Strunk and White's *The Elements of Style*, and Garner's *The Winning Brief*. When you receive a well-written, highly-persuasive brief from opposing counsel, take time to analyze its structure and phrasing.

I am not kidding.

Embrace technology

I do not intend to write a guide to law office management, but I strongly recommend that you make use of the latest technology to have a paperless office.

If you are a minion right now and work at an office that is paperless, get as deep an understanding as possible about how it is all run so that you can replicate it when you start your own law firm.

If you are unfortunate enough to work at a firm run by dinosaurs and you still use reams of paper and rows of filing cabinets, do your best to keep all of the documents you work with scanned and available on your hard drive. (Note: If your office does not have a scanner available for your use, run away as quickly as you can.)

I recommend a paperless office for two main reasons: efficiency and conservation of resources.

The efficiency element should not be underrated. It takes a surprisingly long time to get up from your desk, walk to a filing cabinet, pull out a file, walk back to your desk, and then flip through the file until you locate a letter you sent four months ago. But, if you work in an office that uses paper files, you are likely going to do this multiple times per day.

Compare that to opening your electronic document management software, calling up the client file, and then doing a search by to/from or keyword, and having the scanned document appear on your screen, along with any annotations or notes you have already made about the document and related documents.

And, do not forget that you will need to store a copy of the client file for several years after the matter has ended in case you get sued for malpractice. It is much easier and substantially less expensive to store files in the cloud or on some form of digital media than to store millions of pages of paper in a warehouse.

I also like the paperless technology for its conservation of resources, especially the reduction of paper use. It may surprise some of you that I am concerned about resource conservation, but I am of this world and love this world. I want it to last as long as possible and I want it to evolve at a natural pace. I do not want to see the world dishonored by the prodigal destruction of resources and continued release of greenhouse gases into the atmosphere.

Michel Serres, the French philosopher, argued in *Le Contrat Naturel* that by the late nineteenth century and early twentieth century, mankind crossed out of nature and began to exert the force of geological change in the span of a single lifetime. He meant that what you folks do as a species can have the same effect on the Earth that previously could only have been felt in the span of hundreds of thousands of years. When considered as a whole, humanity now has the power of a god. In fact, humanity's collective power far exceeds my own.

A paperless office environment of course will use some resources, particularly electric energy. But, it also allows you to work from home and not have to drive to the office everyday (assuming your employer is not in the Stone Age about wanting you to come to the office every day so he can conduct surveillance on you). It reduces paper use immensely, and the production of paper, even recycled paper, uses massive amounts of energy and chemicals.

Part 3: Working in a law firm

The hierarchy

There are three stages in your growth as a lawyer: (1) minion, (2) enforcer, and (3) leader. The speed at which you progress, if at all, through these stages is fully under your control.

Most of you reading this book will be in the minion stage, working as a lowly associate in a law firm. (And, isn't "associate" a nicer job description than "minion"?) If you have made the decision to embrace evil, you need guidance on where to go from there. Reading this book lays the essential foundation for you, but you also will need help from a mentor.

As a minion, you need to find someone more experienced with evil to help you practice and learn from your mistakes. Fortunately, this is easy for most lawyers who are working at a law firm. Almost without exception, there will be someone in your firm who long ago embraced evil, even if only in a haphazard, unthinking way. These people are the enforcers and will be found among your law firm's partners.

An enforcer is someone who understands the basics of evil and has learned to prosper from it. In the law firm setting, this is usually a partner who has one, if not many, insurance companies or large corporations as clients. The partner will also have private clients who are charged ungodly hourly rates.

Latch onto this person like a lamprey and learn all you can. If he already has minions and does not seem to have room for you, figure out a way to undermine one of the minions and get him or her fired. Then, fill the vacancy.

The step from enforcer to leader, however, is a difficult one. Not many people make it. Most managing partners of law firms and even founding partners of law firms are simply enforcer-level.

A leader is someone who has perfected his relationship with evil to such an extent that it becomes second nature. This person does not have to think about tactics or strategy anymore; he simply exists and acts naturally. He has become a conduit of power.

To be honest with you – as I have been throughout this book – only a few hundred people living on Earth at any one time rise to the level of a leader. On occasion, those people have been lawyers.

I will not identify any of these leaders for you because I believe that dishonors their great achievements, sometimes attained by deluding hundreds of millions of people. I will say, however, I hold them all in high esteem, both while they are living and afterward.

To become a leader should be your goal, but recognize that the likelihood of you reaching that hallowed status is *de minimis*, as you lawyers like to say. Still, there is no point in starting down this path unless you unhesitatingly work toward becoming a leader.

I can assure you that if you come close to the status of leader, you will receive help from other leaders. They recognize talent and ability and will help you enter their ranks, if you have shown yourself to be worthy.

Keep an enemies list

As you work to build your empire, you will, at times, be forced to swallow your pride and do things for people who do not deserve your respect or obedience. Unfortunately, you must offer those things to them in order to lay the foundation for achieving your goal.

Make note of every slight, insult, embarrassment, mistreatment, thoughtlessness, and foolishness you are forced to endure. Include the name of any person who is the cause. This is your enemies list.

An enemies list serves two main purposes. First, as it grows in length, it will inspire you to achieve your goal more quickly. Look at all the indignities you have suffered because of the ignorance and vanity of others. If this does not motivate you, then you do not deserve the great rewards available for the taking if you simply had the will to seize them.

Second, your enemies list will provide you with a list of targets once your position is fortified. Should you get revenge on all of these people? In my opinion, yes, but at some point it will become a project of diminishing returns. Instead, I suggest you choose the top two or three people from your list. Maybe it is the people who made you suffer the most times, or maybe it is someone who only crossed you once, but that moment caused your greatest suffering.

Find a way to get your revenge without it being traceable to you. Their stunned bewilderment will be a soothing vision for you as you go to sleep each night knowing you have finally and justifiably ruined their lives.

The billable hour

I wish I had invented the billable hour. A truly diabolical idea.

As an associate at a law firm, you will be required to keep track of all of the time you spend on client files, breaking your life into six-minute (i.e., 1/10 of an hour) pieces. There is nothing more demoralizing than breaking your life into tiny packets, especially when you realize that the work you did during each packet of time was utterly meaningless. The billable hour psychologically cripples most people, keeping them obedient and servile.

From the perspective of your employer, another great benefit of the billable hour is that it motivates you to exaggerate how long it took you to complete your tasks. After all, if you don't bill 2000 hours per year, you will miss out on a bonus. But, to bill 2000 hours legitimately, you probably need to actually work 2300 hours (or an average of 46 hours per week for 50 weeks). And, don't forget that 2000 hours is the minimum expected. A "good" associate will bill 2500 or more.

So, here is the deal.

Let your brainless fellow associates yammer on about how many hours they have been billing this month or this year. You are not to pay any attention to billable requirements. Your goal is to learn how to be a great lawyer.

Delegate all the crap work to paralegals and law clerks, concern yourself only with conducting legal research, drafting court pleadings, attending and taking depositions, appearing in court, and communicating with clients.

If your hours don't meet your assigned targets, so what? Let your greedy boss yell at you and threaten to fire you. Put her name on your enemies list, and get back to learning.

Firm events

Attend as many firm events as possible.

There are two reasons you should do this. First, you want to be seen as a team player, even though you are only out for yourself. Your bosses will often attend these mixers, and you want to be seen as a loyal subject, enjoying your lords' exercise of their noblesse oblige.

Second, you will learn all sorts of interesting information about your colleagues and the firm's clients. This is especially true at mixers where alcohol is served. Do your best to sit back, say little, and just listen. Laugh at the appropriate moments, but stay sober enough to remember everything you hear.

After you leave a firm event, take a few minutes to debrief yourself. What did you learn about your colleagues? Did you hear anything you might be able to use in the future to sabotage them with a partner and ease your way up the law firm ranks? Was something said about a particular client that might enable you to form a wedge between that client and your firm such that you can steal that client at a later date?

If you are at all historically-minded, think of these firm mixers like mingling at the court of Louis the XIV at Versailles. Everyone is out to get something, even if they don't know what it is yet. Everything said has layers of meaning. Be suspicious of all. Listen more than you speak.

Through the exercise of restraint and self-control at these mixers, you will earn the respect and admiration of your colleagues. They will see you not getting drunk, not betraying client confidences, and not gossiping about law firm staff and think, "There is a person I can trust to keep my secret."

And, one day, they will walk into your office,

shut the door behind them, and ask, "Do you have a minute to talk?" That is when you know they are about to tell you something good, something you can hold over them or use against them.

Of course you have a minute to talk. Talk is cheap; information is priceless.

Stand up for yourself

If you work as an associate at a law firm, there will come the time when you will be asked to cancel your plans - maybe for the evening, maybe for the weekend - to have the privilege of doing work for a domineering partner or a needy client.

In some circumstances, you must obey this request in order to keep your job. This is especially true when you first begin your job. But, do not allow yourself to be a doormat on which your supposed superiors wipe their loafers.

At some point, you will need to stand up for yourself and say, "Sorry, I can't. I have plans."

The timing of this moment is critical, but it is better to get the timing wrong and get fired than to never have the courage to tell your boss to go fuck himself. Most things simply are not urgent enough to cancel a night with your old college friends or a weekend getaway with your significant other.

As a rule of thumb, if you haven't refused a "request" to upend your life in order to work by the end of the second year of employment as an associate, there is a strong chance you are a coward.

If you ever hope to realize great power and wealth as I have explained it, it is time to grow up. The next time you are asked to do something you were not planning to do, say no and take whatever consequences might befall you.

Freelancing

Most lawyers are either too arrogant to admit this or too stupid to figure it out, but a lawyer is a freelancer. Maybe a highly-paid freelancer, but a freelancer nevertheless.

A lawyer sits around until a random person or company (labeled "the client") comes along needing help with a problem. The lawyer offers to trade her time for dollars (a "reasonable hourly rate," of course) to help the client solve his problem.

You may protest and say you earn a salary and are an employee of a prestigious – or not so prestigious – law firm, not a freelancer. But, think about it. If your boss did not have clients who needed problems solved and who paid by the hour to solve those problems, then your boss would not need to employ you.

So, really, this means that law firms are temporary employment agencies for freelancers.

I do not say this to be pejorative of freelancers or temporary employment agencies. I simply want to make you aware of the precarious position you inhabit as a minion, and suggest you move up the law firm hierarchy quickly.

Or, even better, start your own firm and get paid on a contingency basis. The contingency fee makes it possible to get paid at an obscene hourly rate as compared to the actual time you have spent on a matter.

Or, better still, create a productized legal service that will enable you to move beyond selling your *time* for dollars to selling your *knowledge* for dollars. When you get to that point, you can make money while you sleep or vacation.

Always be alert for better opportunities.

Part 4: On clients

Choice

Somewhere in the musty ethical tomes created by self-important lawyers is a rule that you can refuse to serve a client you find so repugnant that you are unable to provide effective legal services.

I say that if you cannot provide effective legal services because your emotions get in the way, then you are not much of a lawyer. A lawyer should be able to despise someone (e.g., child molester) or something (e.g., strip-mining company) and still provide his or her best efforts.

That said, if you think a potential client cannot *pay* you, then do not take them.

If you are working by the hour, get a substantial amount of money up front. What does "substantial" mean? At least what you think it will cost for the first two months. If you are working on a contingency basis, make sure the client is not insane or belligerent.

This is about you getting paid, achieving your client's goals or vindicating your client's "rights" is merely a side effect.

Insurance companies

If you bill by the hour, the best clients in the entire world are insurance companies. If you can get an insurance company to send you work, take it.

Insurance companies understand that they are evil, and they understand that you are evil. They understand nuance and technicality. They *want* you to find a way to keep them from paying someone who was maimed or disfigured due to the negligence of their insured.

They want you to save them money. Money is the only metric by which insurance companies know how to keep score.

The beauty of insurance companies is that they will pay you several hundred thousand dollars to defend a lawsuit that they could settle for $50,000.

Think of how wonderful this is. Your evil and greed is satisfied while you help insurance companies spread their stain across the world.

But, be aware that the people running insurance companies are cheap bastards, and will do everything they can to pay you as little as possible for your services. If you let them walk on you once, you will be their carpet for the rest of your life.

Don't put up with their bullshit. There is plenty of money in the world for you, but the moment you allow people to disrespect you, the odds of you obtaining that money decrease drastically.

Personal injury plaintiffs

Personal injury plaintiffs are a double-edged sword. Most of them are just whiners who are trying to get paid because they tripped on a crack that everyone else was smart enough to step over. But, some of them have been seriously hurt through no fault of their own and deserve compensation. (At least, humanity believes they deserve it.)

If you decide to work personal injury cases, you will likely have to handle all sorts of pathetic, miserable, shameful, and embarrassing low-dollar cases for years before you start getting the big-value cases where you can earn hundreds of thousands or even millions of dollars in contingency fees. It is a long slog, but probably the best way to ensure great wealth as a lawyer.

If you can do something to shortcut the time between passing the bar and getting your first multi-million dollar case, you will have spent your time well. My advice is that you pick a niche in the personal injury world and tell everyone you meet that you do that sort of work.

Most non-lawyers don't have a clue that a lawyer fresh out of law school is essentially incompetent due to lack of experience. This works to your advantage. Tell enough people that you are a good lawyer and you practice in a certain area, and they will believe it. They will remember your name if anyone ever asks them for a referral to a personal injury lawyer.

Two areas to focus on are brain injuries and wrongful death. Serious brain injury cases are always high-dollar because the victim is going to need expensive lifelong care. Wrongful death cases can also bring in the cash, especially when the deceased was young and earning a lot of money at the time of death.

Pick one of these areas – or another you are interested in – and read as much as you can about that area. For example, if you select brain injuries, then read about concussions, traumatic brain injury, neurology, neuropsychology, and post-injury care. Find as many appellate decisions as you can involving brain injuries and study them. Tell everyone you meet that you do personal injury, specializing in helping victims of brain injuries.

No matter what area you choose as your specialty, reach out to attorneys who have obtained multiple, high-dollar verdicts in that area. Buy them a coffee and ask them how they got their start, get as much detail as possible, and emulate them as best you can. Ask if they can tell you the next time they are in trial so you can watch them work. Try to get a job working for them.

Unless you have a chance to become a partner at an international law firm, the best way to power and wealth as a lawyer is as a personal injury attorney.

Other clients

Other than what I have already discussed, the only other clients worth having are Fortune 500 companies or wealthy career criminals. Everyone else is just too much irritation for not enough money.

Fortune 500 companies have unlimited budgets, but they are also very demanding and difficult to land as a client. Unless you are a partner at a massive law firm, you will never be able to get one of these cash cows as a client.

Wealthy career criminals are wonderful clients because they pay with cash and need your help frequently. They are also a great source of referrals. But, if you fail to deliver on your promises, they have the ability to make you disappear without a trace. I see this as a path too risky for most mortals.

Ignore. All. Other. Potential. Clients.

It may be seen as noble among humans to defend the indigent who have been accused of a crime or to prepare a trust for someone with a tiny, $100,000 estate, but it is not what builds a true empire. If you are serious about choosing the path of evil, you will not serve these people.

The only exception to shunning these substandard clients is when your boss requires you to work with them. As a minion, you have little choice. You might learn something you can use in the future, but it is more likely the only lesson you will learn is that I am right about how wretched it is to serve clients of this ilk.

Rise above your minion status as soon as possible.

Part 5: Keeping up appearances

Dress well

Many young lawyers are caught up in the recent fad of pushing the limits of business casual and the definition of a suit. Many young lawyers want to wear the latest cut of suit, which will look dated and peculiar within a year or two.

This is the wrong approach to legal fashion.

Choose conservative and dark clothing whenever possible. Regardless of the ridiculous, contrived, and gaudy depictions of attorneys being broadcast on television in the twenty-first century, most members of society think more along the lines of a Perry Mason type when they picture a lawyer.

For men, this means a classic cut suit. It can have thin, nearly imperceptible striping, but please no Prohibition Era pinstripes. When you appear in court, wear a suit. Do not wear a sport coat and slacks. Do not wear cheap soft-soled shoes with a suit; leather shoes only. People want their lawyers to look like lawyers, not half-wit slobs.

Women should wear a conservative suit or skirt-suit when appearing in court. It should be tailored, but not skin-tight. Hemline below the knee. Do not show any cleavage when appearing in court. While exposed cleavage may be an advantage when appearing in front of a lecherous old judge, most others observing your breasts popping out of your clothes will either lose respect for you or will be jealous of you. Either way, a detriment. On the other hand, if you are going to a mixer where you might be able to snag some male clients, a little cleavage (keep it tasteful, please) can go a long way.

This is not to say you need to spend thousands of dollars on a wardrobe (with the exception of those of you in Manhattan, Paris or the world's other fashionable cities where those things truly matter).

You can put together a crisp, conservative wardrobe by stalking sales while in law school or by purchasing clothing from a discount retailer and having it well-tailored.

Conservative clothes rarely go completely out of style, so a well-chosen wardrobe will last for many years. And, by then, you will have established your empire and can replace your starter clothes with newer items.

Stay in shape

People respect others who respect themselves. Respect is a fulcrum of power. One of the best ways to demonstrate self-respect is to be in good physical shape.

You may have noticed that when I am not being depicted as a scaly demon, human artists represent me as very muscular human-like creature. In fact, this is my true appearance. I choose to be muscular because men respect it and women admire it.

I am not saying that you need to be a gym rat or a cross-fit fanatic to stay in shape. I simply mean that you should be strong, have good posture, and a healthy stamina created by periodic exercise.

If you are a larger person who always maintains a soft outer layer, that is fine so long as what is under that layer is strong. If you can stand tall and project confidence, you will get respect.

If you are an extremely thin person who does not need to do any exercise to stay thin, people may sense your weakness and pounce. Lift some weights and do some cardio. Eat some meat.

People do judge a book by its cover. You will have a much easier time achieving your goals of wealth and domination if your cover leads to favorable judgments.

Give gifts

The law of reciprocity is well-documented by anthropologists, sociologists and psychologists. Gift-giving is what binds societies and people together. When you give a gift, the recipient of the gift is psychologically in your debt and will want to do something to repay you. The more gifts you give, the more goodwill you create.

There is no need for these gifts to be large. Just be thoughtful.

Always remember the birthdays of your secretary and paralegal. Take them to lunch, buy them a nice bottle of wine or give them a gift certificate to a favorite store they have mentioned.

Get to know your neighbors. Invite them over for a drink or for dinner. If they have children, find out what the kids like and "spontaneously" give them a gift at some point. It should be something small like a book or video game. (Avoid giving anything creepy or pervy, which is especially important if you are a single man.) The parents will think how thoughtful you are, and will remember when someone asks them, "Do you know any lawyers?"

Create a web of obligation around you. You are not doing this because you hope your secretary will give you a gift card on your birthday, but because you want your secretary to like you and recommend you to friends.

And, let us not forget, send gifts to current clients and former clients. You do this to remind them you are thankful for their business and to instill a new sense of obligation in them to send you more business or to send their friends and colleagues to you. (Believe me, referrals are my number one source of new business too.)

But, please, no boxes of chocolate and no

"Holiday Cards." Do something different. Stand out. Make a real impression. For example, send them a card celebrating your country's independence day along with a relevant gift, such as a book of historical trivia about your country with a personalized message written on the inside cover.

And, if you happen to be an associate at a law firm that only pays for partners to send out gifts, spend your own money to send out a few of your own. Pick people who you have worked with and whose business you think you could steal if you ever move to another law firm. Send a thoughtful card or useful book or article to them during a non-holiday period. Be sure to include a business card with your personal cell phone number.

A little thought and originality today will lead to an empire tomorrow.

Sex

Never have sex with coworkers or clients. It is simply too easy and too stupid. Maybe that secretary or file clerk is super hot, but who cares? Do not worry about missed opportunities.

As you increase your power and wealth, your sex life will improve. Trust me.

The only possible exception to this rule is if you need to have sex with your employer in order to get a promotion or with a potential employer in order to get the job in the first place. This expedient can pay dividends if it really is the only way you can get started in the legal profession. (This, for example, may be necessary if you failed the bar exam multiple times or if your grades in law school were below average.)

If you choose the quid pro quo route, know that others will find out and will resent you. It could hamper your ability to progress toward wealth and success. In most cases, these risks outweigh the rewards.

Conclusion

Some of you may be thinking what I am saying here could apply to any number of professions, career paths or entrepreneurial endeavors.

This may be true, but lawyers hold a special place in my heart. This is because lawyers are trained to argue for an idea. It does not matter what the idea is or the moral implications of the idea. A lawyer can be considered a successful lawyer whether she prosecutes murderers or defends them.

This is not true for other professions, such as doctors. A doctor is required to heal. A good doctor heals quickly, while a bad doctor heals slowly. If a doctor hurts someone, the doctor is no longer a doctor, he is a criminal.

But, the supple malleability of lawyers is one of the reasons the general public is suspicious of them. This suspicion grows into outright hatred quite often, as I am sure you know.

None of this is new:

All: God save your majesty!

Cade: I thank you, good people—there shall be no money; all shall eat and drink on my score, and I will apparel them all in one livery, that they may agree like brothers, and worship me their lord.

Dick: The first thing we do, let's kill all the lawyers.

Cade: Nay, that I mean to do.

Henry The Sixth, Part 2 Act 4, scene 2, 71–78

This is how simpletons think, but you have to accept it. I have to deal with this all the time from people who do not understand my role and the role of evil in the universe. Remember what George Burns said.

There are always two sides – at least – to every argument, and without such, totalitarianism and ignorance would reign throughout the world.

Rest assured, I am on your side. I will be watching over you and cheering on your progress.

Recommended Reading

There are few good books on the topic addressed in this book. But, if you are truly interested, please seek out the following books, listed in no particular order (alphabetizing and categorization have always seemed to me crutches of a weak mind):

De kerk van de duivel, (Amsterdam, 1603)

The Rise and Fall of Chen Sheng, Reginald Wainscot (London, 1874)

Night Celebration, Mary Carthright (New York, 1866.)

Enchiridion, Epictetus (c. 125)

An Eyewitness Historie of the Notorious Salem Witch Trials, Anonymous (Boston, 1694)

A minha vida estranha e o terramoto de Lisboa, Fr. Joao de Almeida (Lisbon, 1756).

The 48 Laws of Power, Robert Greene (1998)

Blood Meridian, Cormac McCarthy (1985)

The Prince, Machiavelli (1532)

And don't forget to join me at

satansadvice.tumblr.com.